Beat the Sunset

Michael Lewis MacLennan

Playwrights Canada Press
Toronto • Canada

Beat the Sunset © Michael Lewis MacLennan, 1995

Playwrights Canada Press is the publishing imprint of:
Playwrights Union of Canada
54 Wolseley Street, 2nd floor, Toronto, Ontario, M5T 1A5
Tel (416) 703-0201; Fax (416) 703-0059
E-mail: cdplay@interlog.com; Internet: www.puc.ca

CAUTION: This play is fully protected under the copyright laws of Canada and all other countries of The Copyright Union, and is subject to royalty. Changes to the script are expressly forbidden without the prior written permission of the author. Rights to produce, film, or record, in whole or in part, in any medium or any language, by any group, amateur or professional, are retained by the author. For amateur rights apply to *Playwrights Union of Canada*; for professional rights apply to:
Patricia Ney, Christopher Banks and Associates
6 Adelaide Street East, Suite 610, Toronto, Ontario, M5C 1H6
Tel (416) 214-1155; Fax (416) 214-1150

No part of this book, covered by the copyright hereon, may be reproduced or used in any form or by any means — graphic, electronic or mechanical — without the prior written permission of the publisher except for excerpts in a review. Any request for photocopying, recording, taping or information storage and retrieval systems of any part of this book shall be directed to:
The Canadian Copyright Licensing Agency
6 Adelaide Street East, Suite 900, Toronto, Ontario, M5C 1H6
Tel (416) 868-1620

Playwrights Canada Press operates with the generous assistance of The Canada Council for the Arts, Writing & Publishing Section, and the Ontario Arts Council, Literature Office.

Canadian Cataloguing in Publication Data

MacLennan, Michael, 1968–
  Beat the Sunset

A play.
ISBN 0-88754-549-1

I. Title.

PS8589.H53B56 1998   C812'.54   C97-932615-X
PR9199.3.T44B56 1998

First edition: February 1998
Printed and bound in Canada

Written in memory of Douglas Reed

Author's Introduction

In the same way the play tempts us to make strong initial judgments of its characters which we must subsequently revise, *Beat the Sunset* invites a set of conditioned responses that we have to illness narratives, only to collapse those assumptions in the course of the story. By integrating one disease within its larger social and historical contexts, I have attempted to create a story with wide-ranging appeal, one that staunchly refuses to seem dated.

Illness becomes a metaphor, but one with more constructive uses than the traditional punitive symbolic stigma. I hope instead to use illness as a way to understand our fear of intimate connection of any kind. By investigating how illness confronts our body, we may come to discover how love heals our soul.

So many people contributed to the development of this play, offering support and rigorous criticism. In particular, I remember and thank: Miranda Burgess, Shelley Darjes, Sue Donaldson, Michael Hoppe, Matthew Kynaston, Glynis Leyshon, David Mckay, Brigitte Potter-Mäl and Jay Ruzesky. From the many exceptional research sources I drew upon, I must specifically acknowledge Andrew Nikiforuk's inspiring book *The Fourth Horseman*, which, among other things, introduced me to Jean Bodel.

I am particularly indebted to my friend Michelle Porter, who has been this play's most rigorous dramaturg and its best champion. She showed me how *Beat the Sunset* is in many ways a play about miracles. As we know through accounts chronicling countless corporeal and spiritual transformations, to change one's heart is a more profound miracle than to change one's health.

— Michael Lewis MacLennan

Michael Lewis MacLennan is a playwright and screenwriter who divides his time between Vancouver and Toronto. His most recent play, *Grace*, won the 1996 Canadian National Playwriting Competition and has had productions in Calgary, Vancouver, and Victoria. *Beat the Sunset* has had three productions in western Canada, earning numerous awards. Other plays include *Leaning Over Railings*, *Wake No Clocks*, the collectively created *Coming Out Inside*, and the comic short *Come On!*.

Production History

Beat the Sunset was first presented by Company Epidêmos at the Kaleidoscope Playhouse, Victoria, BC, on August 27, 1993, with the following cast and crew:

MEMORY	Kira Bradley
ADAM CASTORSON	Phil Black
SACHA POLLOCK	Kristian Martin
IRIS CASTORSON	Judith McDowell
DR. THORPE	Kristian Martin
EMMA	Judith McDowell

Director: Michael Lewis MacLennan
Set and Costume Design: David Owen Lucas
Lighting Design: Annie Weeks
Sound Design: Monica Schraefel
Stage Manager: Michael Hoppe
Co-Stage Manager: Karen Visser
Assistant Stage Manager: Maggie Binnie

Beat the Sunset was subsequently revised, workshopped by the Belfry Theatre, and produced at the Belfry Theatre, Victoria, BC, opening November 30, 1993 with the same company.

After final revisions, *Beat the Sunset* was presented by Yorick Theatre at Studio 16, Vancouver, BC, on April 21, 1995, with the following cast and crew:

MEMORY / DR. THORPE / EMMA	Michelle Porter
ADAM CASTORSON	Shawn Macdonald
SACHA POLLOCK	Peter Wilds
IRIS CASTORSON	Beverley Elliott

Co-Directors: Michelle Porter & Michael Lewis MacLennan
Set and Lighting Design: Nik von Schulmann
Costume Design: Mara Gottler
Sound Design: Monica Schraefel
Stage Manager: Sharon Thompson

Production Notes

Scene Changes

Where indicated, music and sounds should be used transitionally. Any blackouts should lead immediately to a scene in another area or lines delivered in the dark. No "down" time should occur during the play, giving a sense of seamless, if non-linear, narrative. While some scene changes may seem difficult and quick, there are numerous ways to create a seamless production, beyond the methods outlined in this script.

Set, sound, lighting, blocking and transition directions are taken from the play's first production, and are not binding — even the contents of the gift in Scene 6 may be changed.

Set Design

The initial design was as follows: A playing area marked off by ten red ribbons in a 22-foot square, suspended from the ceiling and attached to the floor. A triangular "window" juts out down centre-stage, marked off by three ribbons. On stage, a single bed, slightly raked and painted black, with a sheet and blanket, up-stage centre-left. A black bedside table, stage-right of the bed. Two red chairs on either side right of bed. Also, a simple black lectern up-stage right. The stage directions mention windows, doors and walls; these are not to be built, but suggested. Positioning of set elements, particularly chairs, changes from scene to scene. The lectern doubles as a crate which the boys sit on in Scene 7.

Punctuation

Many questions are deliberately punctuated with a period, suggesting a non-interrogative tone of voice.

Intermission

The play has worked successfully with or without intermission. If one is deemed necessary, it should fall between Scenes 6 and 7.

The Characters

MEMORY, *Female*

ADAM CASTORSON, *Male, 28*

SACHA POLLOCK, *Male, 27*

IRIS CASTORSON, *Female, 50*

DR. THORPE, *Female, 30s (played by* **MEMORY**)

EMMA, *Female, 30-50 (played by* **MEMORY**)

Scene One

> *Pre-show,* ADAM *lies in bed, an oxygen mask on. After house lights are down, sound, which resolves into the sound of a heart beating — stylised, a bass note plucked rhythmically, but definitely recognisable. The first lines are delivered in darkness.*

MEMORY It's the first part to live, the last to die.
It's the organ sacrificed,
the part eaten
by the conqueror
for the vital powers
of the vanquished.
The organ
that measures time,
that beats
all the body's blood
through it in a minute.

> *Light slowly up on* MEMORY *sitting on a stool in a black dress. She takes out a red leather glove and holds it in her hand, the outstretched arm away from her body.*

MEMORY Take it out of the body
and it still knows what to do.
The heart has a memory,
an old electricity
charging on, on, on.

> MEMORY *slowly puts the glove onto her hand.*

MEMORY   The heart,
they say,
is about
the size
of a fist.

> *Throughout the scene* **MEMORY** *will play with the idea of the gloved hand as a heart, beating/clenching it over her heart and elsewhere.*

MEMORY   Difference is, they beat
differently. They stroke
differently. They attack
differently. A heart and a fist: they clutch
differently.
They reach for the throat:
different, but not too different.

The first primitive humans
must have felt it,
this insistence of life in their breast.
Did they lie as you do,
on your back to feel and see
the constant leap to the left,
the life
trapped
under a cage of ribs?
Did the heart cease
and teach them what death was?
It told them when enough was enough.

It waited patiently, the heart,
for millennia, passing the time,
always just sipping away
on two ounces of blood.
And all this time, nobody really knew
what the heart
was for.
Sure, it was the seat of the soul,
the centre
of courage and joy and sadness,
of intelligence, vital spirits
and love.

It seemed so ready
to take on anything, any role,
this piece of you.
It keeps you awake at night, wondering.
But how would it feel if your blood were spilling
and you did not know
what this meant?

In 1628
someone found why the heart pumps,
beats its love and devotion
to you right now. Just what it's doing
seventy times a minute.
And the heart says,
It's about time. I am working hard for you;
I won't fail you. I am the machine
which has got us this far.
So take heart.

Right now your blood contains
twenty-five trillion red blood-cells
which, true as the sunset,
give blood its colour.
The colour of speed, of stop.
Of fertility and initiation,
of passion.
The gash through a skull
and the slick of a smile on a clown's mouth.
Catholics are consuming it daily.

Does anybody remember?

These days
the heart's ready, and it's pumping like mad,
and the body's
asking it for thirty litres per minute,
which means all your blood
courses through that heart every ten seconds —
it pumps out a message too fast for decoding.

Does anybody remember?

Now
along with your air and your food,
your chemical instigators,
your immune bodies and waste products,
your body temperature,
your passion, sentiment, and life,
your blood might carry stories
of where you have been.
And it's threatening to tell them.

Now
your blood
just
might
kill.

The instrument of love,
the constant organ of circulation,
from me
to you.
Take,
drink.
The means of transmission
are fluid.
But not tears; no no, my love, not your tears.

> **IRIS** *enters.* **MEMORY**, *carrying the stool, crosses behind her and exits, unseen.*

Scene Two

Lights up on ADAM *lying in bed asleep, oxygen mask on.* IRIS *stands awkwardly, between the door and the bed. Wearing fashionable business clothes and dark leather gloves, she is upset but contains herself.* DR. THORPE *(*MEMORY *in doctor's robe) enters right, carrying* ADAM's *chart.*

THORPE Oh, Hello.

IRIS Yes — Hello. I'm — I'm Adam's mother, Mrs. Castorson. You're his doctor?

THORPE Yes. I'm Dr. Thorpe. I'm happy to meet you, Mrs. Castorson. It's important we touch base.

IRIS I just... I just... would like to know....

THORPE He's in stable condition. The pneumonia is pretty severe for his first bout of it. But he's still fairly strong, he'll fight this through. We have him on antibiotics which will clear up his lungs in about a week to ten days.

IRIS Oh... that's good. I'm sorry I haven't been in earlier. I work quite far from downtown and it's been just crazy. This is — uh, can he hear me?

THORPE No.

IRIS This is his first big illness, isn't it. He's strong.

THORPE	My guess is some chronic symptoms have taken the stuffing out of him the past six months or so. He'll be okay. Does Adam get much help?
IRIS	Well, you see, I just don't know. What I mean is, he only got back in town less than a month ago. We haven't really seen much of one another in the past few years. He can't really handle our lives, I guess. When Adam told us, he was in a pretty bad way. He was living in this one drafty little room in Montreal. We wanted to support him, but not long-distance. So we paid his way back, to Vancouver. Where he'd get good care. We didn't force him back here, Dr. Thorpe. He's got a place near here and we're helping to pay his costs. It's really no trouble. This is a good hospital, isn't it.
THORPE	It's the best in the province for AIDS care, Mrs. Castorson. *(moving to her pressing concern)* Adam has indicated to me that he doesn't get many visitors. You know that visitors and moral support are crucial to how quickly he recovers.
IRIS	Yes, yes, of course. Dr. Thorpe, I hope you'll understand me, when I say this, but he's not the easiest person to be around. I doubt our visits really do him much good anyway. It's hard on everybody. His sister has been in, I know that.
THORPE	Mrs. Castorson, Adam needs a support network that he can count on. We're taking care of him physiologically, but there's much more involved.
IRIS	Right. And we will be there. But I'm sure you can appreciate that my son's illness does not concern people outside the family. He's suffered enough in this city in the past and I've suffered along with him. He doesn't need the indignity of this as well. Cliff, my husband, is a lawyer too. Any whisper of this and he'd start losing clients. It's terrible, but that's life.

THORPE	We expect Adam will be able to leave the hospital in a week to ten days. It may be as early as Wednesday, if you're able to provide partial care to him at your home. We can arrange for a home-care support —
IRIS	Oh, no, no, no. He couldn't stay at our house. I'm sorry, Doctor, but there's just too much going on right now.
THORPE	That's unfortunate for him.
IRIS	Listen. I'm trying. God knows I'm trying to get us all through this terrible, terrible mess. Maybe I'm not always doing the best thing. But please — you just don't know what it would be like for that boy in the house. I'm not abandoning him here — I'm trying to protect him. I'm stuck... in the middle, and I can't do the right thing for anybody. I want him here. In this hospital.
THORPE	*(comforting* IRIS*)* Okay, okay. He'll be okay here.

>THORPE *touches her and surreptitiously looks at her watch.* IRIS *watches* ADAM, *adjusting her gloves.*

IRIS	He's my only son. I don't... I'm not shunning him.
THORPE	Of course not, nobody's saying —
IRIS	I *know* what people say.
THORPE	Well, all right....
IRIS	*(shifting)* So. He's getting better.
THORPE	Yes. *(checking chart)* It looks like Adam has had a restful day.

IRIS   Oh — will he wake up soon? *(short pause as she regards* ADAM*)* I should go. Oh, I've got this card. I'll just... leave it here.

>   IRIS *pulls out a greeting card from her purse and puts it on the bedside table.*

IRIS   Well, thank you for your time, Mrs. — Dr. Thorpe, was it? I'm pleased to have met you. We greatly appreciate the care you and the people here are giving my son. Here's my card, if you need to reach me. I work in real estate.

THORPE   *(accepting the card)* Thank you, Mrs. Castorson.

IRIS   Thank *you*.

>   THORPE *is about to exit.* IRIS *is afraid to be alone with* ADAM.

IRIS   Oh, Dr. Thorpe?

THORPE   Yes.

IRIS   I'm just wondering. When I look at him, I'm wondering... is he losing weight?

THORPE   Yes. He has.

IRIS   Well, he can't lose much more!

THORPE   We're stabilising his weight loss, Mrs. Castorson. Is there anything else —

IRIS   No. Nothing else. Thanks again for your time. I'm sorry.... You are very kind. It's a relief to talk... to someone... who knows.

>   IRIS *exits.* THORPE *exits.*

Scene Three

Lights on SACHA *at lectern.*

SACHA Before we close our first class, I want you to imagine that there is an epidemic in which a disease rapidly weakens the body and shuts down the immune system. This enables other diseases to invade the body. You lie there feverish, soaked in sweat and dying of some combination of diseases specific only to you, preying on your weakened body and soon, killing you.

And this disease seems to have... preferences... about who it infects and kills.

And imagine that the people who die most are pregnant women and children. Pregnant women lose any immunity to the disease. And it takes children five years to develop the antibodies to have a fighting chance against the disease.

And imagine that when it hits men, the fevers reach 104 degrees, temperatures at which sperm cooks. So if you survive, you're probably infertile.

So you have this disease where it's harder and harder for men and women to conceive children in the first place. Then, if the disease doesn't knock off the wife and her fetus, it's likely to press the little one into the ground before he or she is five years old. Makes it hard to have a family. Makes you think — wow, that's some intelligent disease, it sure knows what it's doing.

And if you followed human nature,
if you were a God-fearing type,
you just might think, hey,
this is God's wrath we're seeing,
and it's wrath against heterosexuals.
It's wrath against traditional family values.
It's a sure sign.

The thing is, this disease exists. It has wreaked
havoc for all recorded time, on every continent.
This isn't a fable. Know what it is? Malaria.

Malaria has killed half of the men and women
and children that have ever died on this planet.
Fifty percent of all deaths, ever, have been caused
by malaria. And now, every year, it takes
residence in the bodies of nearly six-hundred
million people, burying one million — almost
the population of Vancouver — one million
African infants each year.

All this from the plasmodium parasite,
the smallest animal on earth.

I wish it were a fable, but it isn't.

> MEMORY *enters down carrying* SACHA*'s satchel. She hands him the satchel and whispers into his ear. As she exits lights change to the hospital, where* ADAM *is still in bed.*

Scene Four

>ADAM *is lying in bed, respirator off, eyes closed.* SACHA, *now in the hospital room, turns up to regard* ADAM. *He stands, shocked and moved by* ADAM*'s state.* SACHA *considers leaving, but returns, tentatively touching* ADAM*'s wrist.*

ADAM   Wanna feel my pulse, big boy?

SACHA   Oh! You startled me.

ADAM   I'm not asleep.

SACHA   No, you're... not.

ADAM   My eyes are just tired, tired of seeing this same old shit.

SACHA   Ah.

ADAM   So go ahead, you got some questions?

SACHA   Ahh, questions?

ADAM   I don't feel like answering, Honey, but don't let that stop you from asking them. Our nurse Emma said you were coming today.

SACHA   *(sighs under breath)* Oh God. *(then)* Adam? *(silence)* Adam?

ADAM   That's me, what's left of me.

SACHA   Can you open your eyes?

ADAM	No.
SACHA	Adam, I think you have me... I'm not the person you were expecting.
ADAM	Oh. *(opens eyes)* You're not the intern? Who....
SACHA	Adam, this is Sacha Pollock. From school? High school?
ADAM	Oh my God. Oh my God. What... what are *you*.... So you're the intern?
SACHA	No, no, I'm... I'm just... here. To visit.
ADAM	Oh. Geeze, this is a hell of a shock.
SACHA	It's been a long time, hasn't it. Ten years.
ADAM	Nine years. Holy shit... you've got guts.
SACHA	Well, not really. This was just a, you know, spur-of-the-moment thing. You've been on my mind. It's really good to see you, Adam. You look swell.
ADAM	Yeah, "swell." Feet swell, glands swell, lymph nodes swell, hemorrhoids swell. Everything's swell, everything but my poor forlorn dick.
SACHA	*(nervous)* Mm, yeah. So... you've been pretty rough then?
ADAM	Oh yes, rough seas for this swollen sack of a body.
SACHA	You want some candies? (SACHA *grabs his satchel and retrieves a box of chocolates*) I brought some chocolates. Very unoriginal, I know, but what else — I couldn't think what to bring. I'm rather inexperienced at this.
ADAM	So am I. A perfect match. *(pause)* Hello, Sacha.

SACHA   Hello.

ADAM   My, my, my.

SACHA   Perfect. Here. *(opening box)* You... you seem okay, though. What do you... I mean... well, what do you *have*, I mean, as an infection.

ADAM   Well, I have pneumocystis carinii pneumonia, a rare parasitic infection which people with AIDS and people with organ transplants receiving immunosuppressant drugs get. And Honey, I didn't get a new organ.

SACHA   Heh. Have you been in long?

ADAM   Yes. But they're probably tossing me out in two days. You caught me in the nick of time. Some intern is going to decide my fate today. That's who I thought you were.

SACHA   Well, I'm glad I caught you. *(nervous chatter)* I've been thinking of you lately and, well, it's just a good thing I came. I've been busy — I'm working as a university instructor now, my first year. History.

ADAM   A history professor at twenty-seven?

SACHA   No, not full professor yet, but tenure track.

ADAM   Sounds like you've been unflinching in the execution of your plans, Sacha. Impressive, especially at such a young age.

SACHA   Most people think I'm a lot older. I don't correct them.

ADAM   In the closet about our age, are we?

SACHA   Well, you have to be.

ADAM   I guess. Actually, I figured you'd be in dentistry. That was the plan... when we were friends.

SACHA   Well, things change. I like history better than mouths. My field is European epidemics. My big class is the, the history... of disease. That's what I'm doing, working on.

ADAM   I like mouths, myself. I'm a mouth man. *(beat)* You want to consult me?

SACHA   Pardon?

ADAM   I asked, do you want to consult me, for your class. Is that why you're here?

SACHA   Oh, hell no.

ADAM   Because I'd charge....

SACHA   No, I told you, I just.... It was a spontaneous act, a simple, spontaneous act.

ADAM   Yeah yeah yeah. So what else is new?

SACHA   Well, I got married four years ago....

ADAM   Right on schedule....

SACHA   But we separated three months ago. No children.

ADAM   *(campy)* Couldn't you figure out how?

SACHA   Adam —

ADAM   Joke! You've done well. I'm surprised. How did you do it?

SACHA   I'm a good planner.

ADAM   Well it couldn't've been brains or creative spark.

SACHA	Seriously, I've always known what I was going to do, and I just ran my life adhering to deadlines. Now I don't know what to plan for. I'm finally in, I achieved my goals, and I can relax so long as my articles are published and my students and colleagues like me. I'm free and clear.
ADAM	How nice for you. But there is that divorce.
SACHA	It's a separation. Listen — the problem is, I realise I don't even like most people around me, and I'm utterly incapable of a truly spontaneous act. I think its potential terrifies me. So here I am, simple. I didn't even know you were sick before I asked after you.
ADAM	Well I'm going blind.
SACHA	What? Really?
ADAM	Well, maybe. I've got herpes in my eye, disintegrating my optic nerve, but they caught it in time. So now I take Acyclovir, which is supposed to stop its progression. If they had waited three more days, I'd be blind in my right eye.
SACHA	That's... lucky.
ADAM	Oh, definitely.
SACHA	I mean... so you're on medication — for how long?
ADAM	Oh, just the rest of my life. Unless the nerve has disintegrated to the point that I'll detach a retina. You know what they say — "It's all fun and games till somebody detaches a retina."
SACHA	Heh.

> SACHA *offers* ADAM *chocolates. They sit silent, eating.*

SACHA   So... I bet you've been around — I mean, I'm sure you've led an exciting life. You went to Toronto after high school?

ADAM   *(pleased with the inventory)* Toronto, New York, Boston, Montreal. I had rich lovers and made fabulous friends everywhere. I even lived in Europe a while. I was a potter.

SACHA   Really! That's good... that's good you stuck with the arts. What do you make?

ADAM   Vessels.

SACHA   Vessels. Yeah?

ADAM   Yeah, empty things. All these vessels I made for people to fill up.

SACHA   Do you still... pot?

ADAM   All that earth, too much to carry around city to city — the wheel, the glazes, the clay....

SACHA   I'd like to see some of your stuff, maybe buy some.

ADAM   Well you can't. I didn't bring any back with me.

SACHA   Nothing?

ADAM   Nothing. I can't imagine you're much of an art buyer anyway, so don't sweat it. *(struck by SACHA's presence)* Jesus Christ. So you drove all the way over from Point Grey to the West End, just to be spontaneous.

SACHA   I didn't drive.

ADAM   What, no sports car?

SACHA   I can't drive, Adam, you know that.

ADAM   Oh, of course. Silly me. Still get fits?

SACHA   I'm on medication.

ADAM   *(a sly challenge)* Of course. How could I forget.

SACHA   *(anger rising)* I don't know. It doesn't go away.

ADAM   No, true. You've got me there. *(pause)* So you caught a *bus* over here just to be spontaneous.

SACHA   Okay, what happened is, I ran into your sister.

ADAM   Huh? Elaine?

SACHA   She told me you were here. So after classes I bought chocolates and sought you out at the hospital. It felt like the first unplanned thing I've done since... well, since I can remember.

ADAM   Why?

SACHA   To see you.

ADAM   Why?

SACHA   I don't know.

ADAM   You don't know why you're here.

SACHA   I'm just here! Adam, what's happened to you?

ADAM   I've changed. Aged.

SACHA   Well, so have I.

ADAM   I'm sure you have, Sacha. All those grown-up things — sex, lust, despair, death. They age us, each just a little bit, a little bite. Bites of an apple, knowledge is. And I'm just one old man nibbling on a core.

SACHA   It's been ten years, Adam, I thought you'd be willing to try —

ADAM Try what? You waltz in here like the handsome prince, exhaust my faltering energies, and for what?

SACHA I didn't think this out!

ADAM Obviously.

SACHA I was wondering if things were worth recovering, something there to retrieve?! You don't have to slop around all this poetic melancholy.

ADAM Oh fuck off.

SACHA Well, that's how it seems, feeling sorry for yourself. That wasn't an easy time for me, either.

ADAM My heart bleeds for you. Sacha, you have no idea what this is like.

SACHA Then let me know. There's a starting point.

ADAM Why the hell should I? You're putting an agenda together before my very eyes. What next, wanna plan my social calendar?

SACHA No I don't want to plan your.... Christ, I'm here to... *talk* to you. Just a fucking visit. It's obviously a big mistake. Well excuse me for showing any interest, any wish to connect, to settle with you. You're sitting on something that happened ages ago, Adam. It eats you. I'm sorry you wrecked this chance. I'm sorry you can't let it go.

SACHA moves to leave.

ADAM Can you?

SACHA Yes!

ADAM   Sacha! Wait. Just.... *(opened by* SACHA*'s threat to leave)* I can't start anything now. There is an effort... that's required... and I can't rise to it. I can't feel future in my blood, Sacha. I can't. You want me to go through all that shit? I don't think I can do it.

SACHA   Well, if you're not starting things.... *(back, fumbling with chocolates)* If you're not growing, you're dying.

ADAM   Right. I'm dying. So stop eating my chocolates and give me one. Look. I appreciate you coming here, taking time off your busy schedule to see me. You'll go back out to your life and your daybook, and I'm stuck in this bed between injections of Pentamidine because there's nobody in this city who will look after me.

SACHA   Nobody?

ADAM   There's no one here. My friends are always on the move, so there's no real "support network," as the counsellor calls it. I never should have come back — it's fucking stupid that I did.

SACHA   You're in prison.

EMMA enters, carrying chart.

ADAM   Yeah, except you, Prince Charming, can just walk into it, invade it, and I have no defences to keep you out.

EMMA   *(crossing)* Well, Sleeping Beauty, I hope you'll allow me into your boudoir.

ADAM   Yes, you get special treatment, Emma. You bring me the only pricks I get now — lovely little needles.

EMMA   Oh, what a sweet guy. Best compliment I've had all day. *(she is hip, busy with medical business)*

SACHA	Hello, Emma. I'm Sacha. I'm an... old friend of Adam's, from high school.
ADAM	Old, *old* friend.
EMMA	Nice you're getting some visitors. Adam, the intern wants to meet with you in the examination room at the end of the hall. You know were it is. And I want to change your bed. So hup out of it.
ADAM	Arrg, I'm convalescing!
EMMA	Then hup with care.
SACHA	Hey... Emma? Would you mind taking our picture? I brought a camera.

        SACHA *quickly opens his bag and gives* EMMA *a Polaroid camera.*

ADAM	Camera?! Some spontaneous act! You're going to release these to *People* magazine. I look terrible.
SACHA	So what. For the archives.

        SACHA *gets on bed with* ADAM. *They ad lib through picture-taking.* SACHA *says "cheese,"* ADAM *says "sex."*

ADAM	Or convert it into a slide for your disease course. Emma, take two. I want one of these.
SACHA	So maybe we could have coffee when you get out.
ADAM	Hear that Emma? When I get out? Ma fella here's gonna wait until da judge lets me out! How romannic! Sure, Sash, I'll see you. We'll have to do something spontaneous, like run naked through a rainstorm.
SACHA	Um, sounds good. Ah, can I get you anything?

ADAM More chocolate —

EMMA Chocolate?!

ADAM Ah! *(exaggerated reaction)* No! You didn't hear that, Emma! No chocolates, none!

> ADAM *begins to cough from his comic flailing. It stops being funny.*

ADAM Makes me phlegmatic or something. Right, Emma? Here, Emma — the covenant of silence. Have a chocolate.

EMMA *(taking a chocolate)* This is a no-no....

ADAM *(to* SACHA*)* This woman is the best.

EMMA Okay, Adam, get down the hall. He's waiting.

ADAM Here, you have this one. *(*ADAM *hands* SACHA *one of the photos)* I look more romantically tubercular in it. *(regarding the one still in his hand)* This one, I just look gawky. Don't want you showing my bad side to my public. *(with affection to* EMMA*)* Why do you think I'm in this remote, hidden spa-village, Honey?

SACHA Now, who would I show?

ADAM Don't know. Show and *tell* was your hobby, last I know, that's all.

SACHA I'll call you.

ADAM Hey, Sash — Sacha?

SACHA Yes?

ADAM *(baiting* SACHA*)* You could bring me some pansies.

SACHA   Uh, sure. *(about to leave, then)* Actually, pansies are good. They're a hardy flower. They are a flowering bedding plant that lasts the winter, no problem. Very tenacious. *(SACHA exits)*

ADAM   Quite appropriate, don't you think, Emma? Hardy pansies to last the winter. Ha!

EMMA   Well I never met a pansy who wasn't hardy!

ADAM   Very true, very true. *(still looking at the photograph, while EMMA tries to move him off the bed)* Hold on — I love watching these things develop.

Scene Five

                    Lights up on SACHA *at the lectern.*

SACHA   In North-East France, in the town of Arras,
a municipal worker and poet
named Jean Bodel stood in his bedroom
alone
in front of his mirror.
He examined again
these large hard swellings
and spots on his skin.
They had begun months ago on his chest
and now they covered his stomach and arms.
His wife was so unsettled
by their ugly appearance
that they made love now only
in complete darkness.

                    Lights up on ADAM, *as Jean Bodel,
periodically, slowly pressing his bare
chest.*

ADAM   Jean Bodel stood by the mirror
pressing his sores with a finger,
because it was the only thing he could do.
He wondered what might have caused
this disfiguration.
As he dressed he knew
he must continue hiding
his blotches with a long-sleeved shirt
and high collar.
In a few months the maculations crept
up his neck. He grew
his hair longer.

Lights up on MEMORY, *centre, in motion of wringing/washing hands.*

MEMORY   When the eruptions had covered his scalp
and were encroaching down his forehead,
it was too much. His wife
could not bear to touch or look at him,
and watchful neighbours had begun
to take notice.
So he went to a doctor who carefully shaved and
dressed the diseased head.
The doctor greased the head in ointments
and while he washed his hands,
whispered a few suggestions
about balms and elixirs and not sleeping
with corrupt women.

ALL   But everybody knew.

MEMORY   There was nothing he could do.
There was no cure.

SACHA   After another week's work, avoiding
the look of his wife and his neighbours
and his mirror,
Jean Bodel could not deny it anymore —
he was destined to leave
to live separated from his family, friends and home,
destitute and shunned.

The year was 1202.

Passing candle to ADAM.

SACHA   Jean Bodel had leprosy.

MEMORY   *(with a Bible)* Jean Bodel was ritually separated
from his town, in the *separatio leprosarum*.
The separation ceremony for lepers
was a funeral mass.
The church was draped with black cloth,
and poor Jean Bodel arrived on a bier
covered in a black shroud.

ADAM *(with lit candle)* He listened
to his own funeral. After the mass,
Jean Bodel stood *(kneeling)*
in a freshly-dug grave, holding a candle...

IRIS *(entering...)* While his family and friends flocked
around the grave
daring to look down to him,
daring to face
his deviance, his difference,
the ugliness of this lengthy,
incurable illness before them.

MEMORY They were supported by a mistranslated book
called the Bible,
which argued it normal and pious to shun lepers
as you would flinch
from any obvious symbol of God's wrath.
The priest dropped three spades full of earth
on Jean Bodel,
saying, in French of course,
"Be dead to the world, be reborn to God."

ADAM The priest then read the Rules of the Dead.

MEMORY *(reading from the Bible)* "I forbid you ever
to enter churches or to go into a market
or a mill, or a bakehouse,
or into any assemblies of people.
I forbid you ever to wash your hands
or even any of your belongings
in spring or stream of water of any kind.
I forbid you ever henceforth to go out
without your leper's dress,
so that you may be recognised by others.
I forbid you to have intercourse with any woman,
except your wife.
I forbid you to touch infants or young folk,
whosoever they may be.
I forbid you henceforth to eat or drink
in the company except that of lepers."

	Then, as an example, the priest tossed the first donation into the alms bowl.
SACHA	The congregation followed: Clink into the alms bowl and then turning away.
	Others provide stylised sounds of clinking as they walk off.
ADAM	Clink of a coin, then turn and walk away. Clink, his wife. Clink, his two children turned. Clink, his mother. Clink, his friends and neighbours. Clink, everyone turned. Clink, until Jean Bodel was left alone to hoist himself out of the grave and journey with his bowl and its contents rattling to the leper house nearby.
SACHA	Lepers lived in leper houses, known as lepresoria, lazarettes, or, as we know them, hospitals. Thanks to leprosy, we had the invention of the hospital, which was a substitute for this ritual expurgation symbolising passage from this world into the next. A place to segregate, house and hide the sick. By the thirteenth century, every village had one. Jean Bodel remained in the leprasorium for most of his remaining eight years. He was often too afraid to venture outside — leper-bashing was popular then as it was everywhere in times of social frustrations, of famine, social upheaval and natural disasters.

ADAM *holds the candle under his face while the lights dim around him.*

His nose began to erode, his lips and tongue swelled, his skin began to hang in folds. His eyebrows disappeared, his hands and feet turned into claws, and his voice changed to a hoarse whisper. Finally, as lepers lose all sensation in the skin and muscles, Jean Bodel became prone to accidentally knocking off his knuckles and toes.

ADAM *drops the candle and* SACHA *knocks on the lectern.*

SACHA Doctors still don't know how leprosy is spread, although in 1874 Armauer Hansen
found a bacteria
mycobacterium leprae, which is
somehow associated.
The disease seems to prey
on faltering immune systems....

Blackout.

Scene Six

                IRIS *sings from blackout, perhaps over previous sound cue.*

IRIS   Happy Birthday to you
Happy Birthday to you
Happy Birthday, dear Adam
Happy Birthday to you.

                ADAM, *in bed, is woken by the singing.* IRIS *stands holding a large wrapped box.*

IRIS   Happy Birthday, Adam. Here's your present.

ADAM   Wow, you're here early.

IRIS   I took an hour off work to get here before rush hour. The traffic downtown is just crazy. I think I know where the motivation for those drive-by shootings comes from. *(laugh)* I tell you, I was out for blood.

ADAM   Well, it's nice to see you.

IRIS   So here's your present. You're looking much better. Did you get my card from last week?

ADAM   Yes, thanks. Sorry I was asleep.

IRIS   That's no problem. You needed the rest. You're looking much better. You're feeling better? You've got a great doctor, that Dr. Thorpe. I met her last week. Go on, open your present.

ADAM Is Dad coming in? Maybe I should wait.

IRIS Oh, I don't think he'll make it. Remember that Hong Kong girl who was abducted? He's in court today defending the "alleged abductors." I thought you knew he was on that case. It's a big one — he was on the news.

ADAM I don't watch TV, Mom. Why should I know that?

IRIS What, take an interest in someone else's life for once?

ADAM Oh yeah and he's raking in the bucks defending some kidnappers five-blocks away? That's a long trek for a visit.

IRIS Your father is very busy, Adam. I never even see him. Open your present.

ADAM Is Elaine planning on dropping in?

IRIS Adam, how in God's name am I supposed to know? She's busy. I'm not responsible for getting her here. If she wants to come, she will.

ADAM I just asked you a simple question.

IRIS Well, she's working. It's just five o'clock now, and she'd have to pick up Trevor from daycare. And the traffic is terrible on Fridays — crossing the bridge was hell. Crazy rat race. Did I tell you we're going to Reno in April? With Ron and Tracy. Just for five days. Play some blackjack. Ron had a tumour — you know? Well, it's just amazing what they can do these days. They — what's it called — they kind of zapped it with a laser until it disappeared; he didn't even need surgery. Incredible. So I guess Ron feels like he's on a winning streak and who can blame him? And you know their little Anna? Well, she's getting married!

ADAM	So….
IRIS	So open the present!
ADAM	The present, yes. Mom, I've been thinking. I want to go to France.
IRIS	You've already been to France.
ADAM	And I want to go back. Before I can't go anywhere.
IRIS	It's not very healthy. For you to travel right now.
ADAM	Why not? People have been travelling to the south of France for centuries for their health. I need to get out of here.
IRIS	You're getting out of the hospital tomorrow, aren't you? I talked to Dr. Thorpe.
ADAM	I need to get out of Vancouver.
IRIS	You just got here! Adam, we just flew you here four, five weeks ago! When did you decide this?
ADAM	Today. Last night.
IRIS	Oh, and you're already so sure you want to go?
ADAM	I know I want to go to France! Don't try to tell me what I do and don't want.
IRIS	I suppose you'd want us to pay for your trip.
ADAM	I have a little saved, but not enough for a trip.
IRIS	I thought you had no savings, Adam. That's what you said when you called us.

ADAM   Mother, okay, I have virtually no money. I'm a fucking pauper compared to you guys. You could go to Europe any time you like, so don't blame me for you not going.

IRIS   You're never happy anywhere — flit here, flit there, never settle down. When are you going to have a home?

ADAM   A home. Yes, well, I haven't really found it too easy to make a home. My first one wasn't the kind of model I'd want to follow.

IRIS   Oh really, and what was so terrible about it? Did we screw you up, is that it? Did we abuse you? Neglect you? Did we... hurt you in any way? Did we? No. We loved you. We gave you a happy childhood, a good home. Which you seem to have forgotten in favour of your morbid revisions, your cynicism, and your cosmopolitan Atlantic friends.

ADAM   I'm talking three weeks. A small trip to France. Visit a few friends, settle things. The last time! I've never asked this of you before. I've lived ten years without a cent from you.

IRIS   What about art school in Montreal. What about when you come back and want to go on another one of your trips. When will this stop?

ADAM   Who the fuck knows? I'll probably be dead in a few months, so you won't have to worry about it.

IRIS   Adam! Stop that, you're getting better. I can see it.

ADAM   Oh, and I'll be cured by Dr. Thorpe the miracle worker in no time.

IRIS   Well, maybe if you got a better attitude —

ADAM Just shut up about my attitude, okay? My attitude is perfectly fine and natural. I'm dying and I'm trapped and I can't breathe. I can't do anything I want.

IRIS You're sounding like a child. *(before he can answer)* All right. I'll talk it over with your father. We'll look things over.

ADAM begins to get out of bed.

IRIS What are you doing?

ADAM I'm getting out of bed.

IRIS Where are you going?

ADAM I'm standing up! Jesus, I can get out of bed, you know.

IRIS Don't you want your present?

ADAM I want to go to France.

IRIS Okay! I get your message! And I don't want you in France. I want you here. To help you.

ADAM How?

IRIS I don't know.

Silence. They tire of the fight. IRIS sees the photograph on the table.

IRIS Who's this? *(picks up the Polaroid)* Who's this in bed with you?

ADAM Oh. *(inaudible)* Shit. *(thinking quickly)* That's... a photo Emma took for me yesterday. You know, that great nurse? Have you met her? She's my favourite person on the ward.

IRIS So you do get visitors. Is he... an old friend?

ADAM   Not really.

IRIS   You know, he's... he looks.... *(she knows)* Adam, who is this.

ADAM   *(pause)* It's Sacha.

IRIS   Sacha Pollock? You're joking.

ADAM   Elaine ran into him and she told him.

IRIS   She what?

ADAM   Yesterday.

IRIS   What did he want.

ADAM   I'm not sure. To see me.

IRIS   And tell the whole goddamn world, I bet.

ADAM   Mother, I doubt it.

IRIS   Oh this is not good.

ADAM   Mother, he just visited. Old times' sake. I doubt he'll be back.

IRIS   And what if he does — did you tell him where you live?

ADAM   Elaine told him.

IRIS   What? I've got to call her tonight. *(pulls out her purse and makes a note in her daytimer)* And what if he does visit?

ADAM   Well, maybe I'll be in France.

IRIS   Yes. Maybe. Christ, Sacha Pollock. What's he doing?

ADAM   He's a professor. Lectures on diseases.

IRIS	Professor? Oh, how fitting. He'll use you in one of his lectures, no doubt.
ADAM	*(smile)* That's what I said.
IRIS	So what did you tell him?
ADAM	Oh, just my sordid life story.
IRIS	There it is, that capricious, I-dare-you way you have of shoving your personal details down everybody's throat.
ADAM	Shoving? Now, there's only one personal detail I've shoved down a number of throats, Mother. I think I can protect myself.
IRIS	See? There you go. That's exactly what I mean. It's violent the way you work at upsetting me. Do you do this with everybody?
ADAM	Be myself? Yes.
IRIS	I can't believe you'd want to tell him anything, that's all.
ADAM	Did Ron hide his tumour from everyone? Keep it hidden in his breast pocket so nobody would know?
IRIS	That's different.... He got better. I can talk about that.
ADAM	And I can't talk to one old friend?
IRIS	Oh, now he's an old friend, is that it? Just to spite me.
ADAM	Why would I spite you? What for?! You're the one punishing me!
IRIS	What...?
ADAM	For being a faggot.

IRIS Adam! I will *not* —

ADAM You've cut me out of your life, and the only way I'm allowed in is if I'm quiet and dying and do as I'm told. You're trying to get back at me for being gay.

IRIS Adam, Adam, I'm not. I don't have any anger against you.

ADAM You don't feel anything, is that it? Ten years you've built up a wall from me. A wall built by the blood and guts of your other child. She gives you a bittersweet pleasure by bearing you a grandson, but one born around the fringes of socially acceptable behaviour. I know, in your time being gay was taboo — well, so was being a single mom. You've accepted Elaine only because your friends have — they see nothing wrong in her life, so you can find it in your heart to love her with no personal risk. And me? You've killed me from the topic of any conversation you might have. I get a few phone calls —

> IRIS *ad libs through* ADAM's *lines, stopping before the end of "Happy Birthday":*

IRIS It was always impossible to track you down — We'd didn't know what city you were in, what side of the Atlantic — We'd go for months without a phone number for you — We wouldn't have a number for you! — *(etc)*

ADAM Some forced birthday message on the machine:

Happy Birthday to you
Happy Birthday to you
Happy Birthday, dear Adam
I'll call you next year.

Now I'm back, and I get pretty much the same treatment. And I'm sick of it. I want to make peace.

IRIS   Well it sure doesn't show.

ADAM   You won't let me take my defences down! I would like to just... rest, not have you wrestle everything I say into the ground.

IRIS   You left....

ADAM   I left because you couldn't handle me being here, could you. I was too embarrassing to you, to the women you golfed with and played bridge with. I went so there would be nothing at stake for you loving me, and still you couldn't do it.

IRIS   You left because you wanted to. You always were tugging away — the minute you could, you were out the door. I knew that's what would happen, no matter how hard I tried. And I tried. I wanted to help you then, but you just slipped away. And what am I left holding? What am I holding together here? I do all the maintenance in this family, the housework to keep relationships scrubbed bright and intact. You can all rail against me, and judge me all you like. You can all be lazy in your roles as son, father, as grandfather, sister. Because I kept you to task. I'm not doing it anymore. *(beat)* Adam... you know I....

ADAM   What.

IRIS   Well you were always... throwing things at me. Those articles you'd send us, on your art, where you publicly state your... gayness.... And what kind of show was that in... in....

ADAM   In Boston.

IRIS   Boston! With those... phallic things you made? Your father nearly died.

ADAM: That was a good show. That was my only solo exhibition.

IRIS: It was so hostile. I know you're gay, Adam —

ADAM: I didn't do it to be hostile to you! God, don't flatter yourself.

IRIS: Calling yourself a — a faggot in press, we need to hear that?

ADAM: I *am* a faggot, Mom! And proud of it.

IRIS: Do you know what that does to me? Do you know? "Faggot" — like a slice through my gut, straight to my womb when I hear that. The word cuts me, burns me. Why are you blaming me?

ADAM says nothing while his mother breaks and then composes herself. Underlying tension carries through until the end of the scene.

IRIS: I've got to go.

ADAM: Emma's usually here with dinner by now.

IRIS: We're having the Strongs over tonight.

ADAM: Oh. Well, you better hurry then.

IRIS: Yes. And I'll tell your father you said hello.

ADAM: Did I?

IRIS: *(forcing herself to ask)* Shall I drive you to the apartment tomorrow?

ADAM: I'll take a cab.

IRIS: *(leaving money on the table)* Fine. Here's some money, then, for groceries too. The apartment's all cleaned up. Call us if you have any problems.

ADAM   Goodbye then.

IRIS   I hope you like the present.

                         IRIS *exits.* ADAM *stands holding himself.*

ADAM   "Hope you like the present."

                         Lights slowly dim on ADAM.

                         Intermission.

Scene Seven

>ADAM *(as 14)* and SACHA *(as 13) enter, carrying flashlights, wearing winter clothing, mittens, handkerchiefs around their necks.* ADAM *may carry a blanket.*

ADAM You sure you're allowed?

SACHA Yeah, we're not doing nothing wrong.

ADAM Well maybe we should just tell your Mom and Dad we're down here.

SACHA Don't sweat it, man.

ADAM I am not sweating it, Sash. It's too fucking cold down here.

SACHA Man, where's the light?

ADAM How am I supposed to know? It's your crawlspace — you don't even know where the light is?

SACHA Oh shut up, Adam, or I'll punch you.

ADAM Like to see you try — y'can't even find me!

SACHA *(flashlight on* ADAM*)* Found you.

ADAM Ahh! You got me!

>*A mock death.* SACHA *ignores* ADAM, *goes to crate, pulls out cigarettes.*

ADAM   It's freezing in here.

SACHA   Come sit over here.

                   ADAM sits beside SACHA

SACHA   You know hypothermia? You know what they do if you've got it?

ADAM   Stick you in a jacuzzi?

SACHA   *(playing with the cigarette and matches)* No way, your veins would explode, 'cause they'd be almost frozen. All your flesh would cook and you'd feel like you were being boiled alive.

ADAM   Gross!

SACHA   Yeah. So what they do is, they put you in bed with everybody under tons of big blankets and you sip warm liquid, but just a bit at a time. And you snuggle up with all these warm bodies, and slowly you warm back up again!

ADAM   Wow. Neat idea.

SACHA   *(he finally lights a cigarette)* Man is it cold. God it's cold.

ADAM   Get closer. It's not that bad.

SACHA   Fuck it's cold. *(they are huddled beside one another now)* Want one? *(offers cigarette)*

ADAM   Uh, sure. (SACHA *hands him the lit cigarette and lights himself a new one)* Thank you. I like it when you light them.

SACHA   I love lighting these things. It's like the best part. I get them from Willie's brother. Do you think he's a fag?

ADAM   Who, Willie?

SACHA   No, his brother, stupid. Willie said his brother tried to kiss some guy, his cousin!

ADAM   I don't know, I never thought about it.

SACHA   Doesn't take much to tell, he's such a faggot. Can you imagine kissing a boy? How gross.

ADAM   I don't know... I mean, it's a good thing girls don't think so!

SACHA   Ha! you're right. Good thing. I'd like to kiss Holly Sutherland. She is such a babe, I get a boner when I think about kissing her.

ADAM   Yeah, she's cute.

SACHA   Hey, who gives you a boner?

ADAM   Oh, different girls. Depends on my mood. Can I have another cigarette?

SACHA   Why don't you finish the one you already got?

ADAM   Just that I'll need another one pretty quick. I — I think I'm getting addicted.

SACHA   Already? Wow, you better watch it. Here. Light it off your other one. When they do that it's called chicken-fucking.

> ADAM *coughs. They smoke.* ADAM *shines the flashlight around them.*

ADAM   So you wanna do it?

SACHA   I don't know, it's so cold, Adam.

ADAM   Well so what?

SACHA   You sure it's safe?

ADAM   Yeah, I read it in a book.

SACHA What book?

ADAM Oh, just some novel. Took place on the prairies when they were pioneers.

SACHA You read weird stuff. Did they say how?

ADAM Yes... they did it by a river.

SACHA Well this ain't no river!

ADAM Fuck, that don't matter. So take off your mittens.

SACHA Is there something we should say when we —

ADAM Definitely. Sure, let's just let it come to us, though.

SACHA Swell. Here. *(SACHA offers his hands)*

ADAM Hold still.

>   ADAM *reaches into his pocket and brings out a knife, holding it close to SACHA's right wrist.*

SACHA Wait — will this leave a scar?

ADAM Naw, it's only a small cut.

SACHA Just be careful, okay?

ADAM Yeah. Here goes.

SACHA Oh God, I hate pain.

ADAM Oh, like and I love it. Okay.

>   ADAM *cuts SACHA's wrist.*

SACHA Ow! Did you get it?

ADAM Yes, y' baby. Now quickly, you do mine.

ADAM takes off his mittens.

SACHA Okay, here goes.

He cuts ADAM's wrist. They look at their wrists.

ADAM Now we wrap in the handkerchiefs. Did you sleep with yours around your neck?

SACHA Yes, never took it off till now.

ADAM Okay, now we wrap the handkerchiefs....

SACHA Your Mom won't get mad, will she?

ADAM Naw, I can just wash it when I get home.

SACHA Okay, okay.

Pause.

ADAM Do you think it's working?

SACHA Yeah, I think I can feel it! *(he thinks to himself)* So, what do we say? Ummmmm.... *(making the oath up as he goes along)* Okay now... I solemnly swear...

ADAM I solemnly swear...

SACHA To be blood brothers...

ADAM To be blood brothers...

SACHA With my best friend...

ADAM With my best friend...

SACHA Adam...

ADAM *(giggles)* Sacha...

SACHA Until we die.

Beat the Sunset / 47

ADAM   Until we die.

SACHA   His blood is in me...

ADAM   His blood is me — in me...

SACHA   And my blood is in thine.

ADAM   And my blood is in thine.

SACHA   By the power vested in us...

ADAM   The power vested in us...

SACHA   Forever and ever...

ADAM   Forever and ever...

SACHA   The end — *until* the end.

ADAM   Until the end. And I promise...

SACHA   I promise...

ADAM   To be honest and true...

SACHA   To be honest and true...

ADAM   And never let another friend...

SACHA   And never *ever* let another friend...

ADAM   Take your place.

SACHA   Take your place.

ADAM   There.

SACHA   There. Alright!

They hold together for a beat.

ADAM   Do you think we should, I don't know... seal the bond?

SACHA	How, like a kiss?
ADAM	Yeah, that would do. Just a kiss of friendship, like they do in France.
SACHA	How's that?
ADAM	One on each cheek... then one on the mouth. They do it in Quebec, too.

Pause. They kiss thrice.

SACHA	S-so you wanna go now? I'm getting kinda cold.
ADAM	Oh, yeah. Just wait — the band-aids.
SACHA	Oh, good thinking.

ADAM pulls bandages from his pocket and puts them on SACHA and himself.

ADAM	So you've never been blood brothers with anybody before, have you?
SACHA	Nope, and I never will.
ADAM	Good, 'cause that's the thing. You can only do it once, y'know. It's a once-in-a-lifetime thing.
SACHA	Yeah, and we're not gonna... this is safe, right?
ADAM	Safe as can be. It's only blood, Sacha, it's not like we traded spit.

They gather their things.

SACHA	Right. Uh, Adam... this is also a secret, right?
ADAM	Yeah, like wishes have to be secrets.

They run off past MEMORY, whom ADAM discovers with his flashlight.

ADAM	Sacha?

Scene Eight

MEMORY *(delivered to audience)*

There's this link you hadn't reckoned on,
this virus which tethers eros to thanatos,
bounds love with death.

If he bleeds, you don't want to touch him:
If she bleeds, you don't want to touch her:
You fear the fugitive she's harbouring
in the Braille of her blood.

So you want bodies that are firm, hard,
impervious.
You want perfect, unblemished skin,
you want something which denies the mess
coursing through you both.
You want sex without secretions.
Your body is now armour, clenched against death
and against love's touch.

But inside, there's an instrument of love,
a constant organ
of circulation
driving a clean slice
across time.

>   MEMORY *crosses to the gift, opens it, bringing out a beautiful blanket which she cradles like an infant, turning to fling it across the bed, just as* ADAM *sits upon it.*

Scene Nine

>*Lights up on* ADAM *alone, sitting up on the bed. He pulls out a make-up case which he uses to change his features into a less healthy, gaunter appearance: more pale, hollow eyes and cheeks, pasty mouth.* ADAM *applies the make-up as if he is accustomed to the act, as one might put her/his makeup on every morning, vanity turned on itself.*

ADAM I love good calves. Best part of a leg, I think. Many times I've followed a good set of tanned, smooth calves in shorts and low socks, ten blocks out of my way. Didn't matter if I was on foot or on my bike.... Bicycle couriers — they are consistently the best, even wearing those long-johns under their shorts in the winter, in rain; you can still see those bulbs of muscle underneath, pumping down, waiting for spring, to bud out.

And what's wrong with seeking a little beauty in the middle of the grotesque, flabby cities I've lived in? What's wrong with pursuing a few knots of beauty on firm legs, lurking ten paces behind them? They fortified me. As I rode or walked back to my own route, they fortified me, kept me going. Kept me sure of the track I was on.

There are things my body has lost. There's always muck on my lips, on my tongue. I brush my tongue raw, but the yeast waits in the cracks and in a few hours, it's covered everything again. It's a stupid battle. Who'd want to kiss these lips?

> ADAM *places calamine lotion on his chest — blotches to suggest shingles, blisters.*

ADAM

I was never that big. People used to warn me about catching some tropical disease, that I couldn't handle the weight loss. But I'm okay. It's just this neck. *(holding it)* I really loved the simple material of my neck — lean, firm, nothing wasted. It mocks me now, every time I look in the mirror. Thin enough? Thin enough? Like some erogenous zone gone bad, gone to seed, all thinning out.

My hair is thinning too, like mad. And the worst dandruff embarrasses me. My body is leaving me via my head. Scales and hairs. My beautiful hair.

I used to have great calves. Worked so hard to get them, too. And you know what? They were the first thing to go.

Lights down on **ADAM**.

Scene Ten

Lights up on MEMORY, *who has entered with a closed umbrella.*

MEMORY
Years back, in his city flats at night,
the telephone's ring would punch his gut awake
until sightless, he'd roll over
and answer
the call whose dark hour already betrayed
the urgent message of endings.
He'd lean his ear to hear the static voice
attenuated, and grasp the loss
of some ex, another friend dead. Clink.

The calls came regular then,
every eight weeks or so,
leaving him chilled, to lie in darkness
tracing his own history, the sex,
measuring the mounting odds against him,
the risks of the heart he had taken
with each dead man.

He'd sink into the mattress
then roll back
to peck the chin of a new, invisible lover.

Opening umbrella.

MEMORY
When he finally slept, a dream would open
of walking wet
streets slicked smooth
for dangerous
driving
and finding an old love, a first love.

By then, Adam's body
would be so beautiful
it would become invisible, everything lost
but desire's firm glow.

In a rain of mercy
the two men would meet
and their bodies would recover
memory's touch, taste and smell.
Recover memory's old senses,
pleasures discovered when nothing was tainted.
And then,
he'd wake.

> *Sound suggesting rain.* MEMORY *brings the open umbrella down in front of her.* SACHA *enters, receives the umbrella which* MEMORY *then drenches before exiting.*

Scene Eleven

Lights up on ADAM *in bed, shirt off, blanket over him, mittens on. Perhaps pansies on the bedside table. Enter* SACHA *with umbrella and bag of groceries.*

ADAM   Hey! Will you quit just storming into my home like that?

SACHA   Well, friend, the door was open.

ADAM   I could have been in a compromised position.

SACHA   Oh, who with?

ADAM   I could have been jerking off or something.

SACHA   Then you would have locked your door.

ADAM   Or you would have got a big thrill.

SACHA   Jeez, I'm soaked. It's pissing down.

ADAM   What do you have there, sex toys?

SACHA   Sorry, they weren't on the list. I decided to skip office hours and make us brunch. You like brie and asparagus omelettes?

ADAM   Don't think I've ever had one. Skipping classes now, are we?

SACHA   No, office hours. Nobody ever shows anyway. What's the matter — frostbite?

ADAM	Not very prudent for a tenure-track instructor, is it?
SACHA	Listen, do you want some food? You eaten yet?
ADAM	No.
SACHA	It's nearly eleven and you haven't eaten?
ADAM	I had a craving for a brie omelette, but didn't have the ingredients. I haven't really shopped since the last time you were over — which was some time ago? Brie and asparagus, la-di-da! You must be gay.
SACHA	Faggot.
ADAM	Breeder. I have shingles.
SACHA	Shingles?
ADAM	It's driving me crazy. Every way I lie I'm in pain. It's like this shiver, sliver, razor's edge between pain and torturous itches. I'm dying to scratch, and then I scratch and I'm thrown into convulsive pains. *(raises his hands)* These protect me from despoiling myself.
SACHA	Convulsive pains. Well you suffer nobly. Some food? I'll cook if you talk.
ADAM	Yeah, sure. First, how about... well, first could you put calamine lotion on my back? It's mostly along my spine, you'll see the blisters. I have one on my dink. Y'ever tried jerking off with calamine lotion? Here. *(tossing the lotion)* Give it a try.
SACHA	Blisters? Uhh, shouldn't you have a shirt on or something?
ADAM	Probably.
SACHA	Should I, uh, wash my hands or....

ADAM You won't catch anything. You've got to be pretty fucked-up to get shingles.

SACHA Maybe... if there's some plastic gloves?

ADAM In the bedside table. Courtesy of Mother, bless her paranoid little heart.

SACHA Well you could catch something from me, too.

ADAM Yeah, right. I'm hoping to get a whole latex outfit I can put on for Mom's visits. Sit and sweat in it for forty minutes once a week. *(leaning forward in bed, exposing his back to SACHA)* Like a big condom.

SACHA So I just put.... *(looking at ADAM's back)* These look pretty mean, Adam.

ADAM So be careful.

SACHA Have you shown these to anybody?

ADAM I'm showing them to you. You're not the first, but be gentle, big fella. They're shingles. I'm miserable. I'm on drugs. They'll go away, I suppose. *(SACHA touches ADAM's back)* Ow! Where you been?

SACHA Mid-terms. I had to mark ninety papers.

ADAM Couldn't you pace yourself over the course?

SACHA I like to get them done in one go. You need a context, and that comes from a concentrated period of time. It only took me a week.

ADAM Ow! Be careful.

SACHA You're looking better, on the whole.

ADAM No I'm not, I look miserable.

SACHA   Well, you look better than before, since you've recovered from the pneumonia.

ADAM   I still have the glands and throat and thrush.

SACHA   Well take it one thing at a time.... You got over the pneumonia.

ADAM   And now I got shingles.

SACHA   This isn't as bad. This is a temporary setback, right?

ADAM   Right. And then something else comes along, and then something else, until my poor body is so battered and weak, it just gives up. People can die of shingles, you know.

SACHA   Not that often.

ADAM   No, but it can happen.

Pause. SACHA *applies calamine.*

SACHA   There's a play on at the Playhouse; it opened last night and a colleague said it's really good. I thought maybe you'd like to go tonight? It's —

ADAM   Hello? Reality check? Can you see me?

SACHA   Yes, and I thought maybe you'd like to go out and do something instead of lying in bed.

ADAM   Well, let's just see how I feel.

SACHA   I should make reservations, that's all.

ADAM   Then maybe you should ask somebody else. One of your many girlfriends? Just pull out your little black book — OW!

SACHA   Sorry.

ADAM   You meant that.

SACHA Well be nice. I wanted to do something with you, as a friend.

ADAM Your friend is sick in bed.

SACHA You've been in a bed for four weeks now. You've probably lain there ever since you came home from the hospital.

ADAM That's 'cause ever since I recovered from pneumonia, I got shingles. I'm in pain!

SACHA And you could lie alone tonight in pain, or you could sit in a theatre with me tonight, in pain. The choice is yours.

ADAM *(sarcastic)* Thank you.

SACHA *(stops applying the lotion)* Look, I can't take away your pain, Adam. I'm doing what I think I can, trying to help.

ADAM Why? Why do you bother? What the fuck are you doing here anyway? You say you're straight, you say you've no ulterior motives. You don't even know me. You wanna be in my will, is that it? There's nothing to give.

SACHA I do know you, Adam.

ADAM Oh, you've seen me a few times and you know me better than anybody.

SACHA Yeah. I understand you more deeply than anybody does. I haven't known you since you moved, but I knew you when you were... becoming. An adult. Before this armour was up. You called me your best friend. You called me your brother — or do you want to forget that? We were a common front.

ADAM That's a lark.

SACHA   What about our secrets, the plans we'd make together, our conspiracies, the books we were going to write together. I remember camping with you and sharing our fear of the darkness, shivering together... like... like....

ADAM   Like lovers.

SACHA   Sure, yeah, sure.

ADAM   We *were* lovers.

SACHA   We were not lovers.

ADAM   We were lovers, Mr. Denial, and if you can't admit that, then I don't know what you're doing here. It's not such a big thing. I'm sure your ample masculinity could deal with it.

SACHA   You call it what you want, and I'll call it what I want.

ADAM   It happened, and you want to forget it.

SACHA   My memory is just as valid as yours, Adam.

ADAM   Much more selective. *(tired)* Oh, Christ.

> SACHA *has returned to gingerly massage* ADAM*'s neck.*

ADAM   Mmm.

SACHA   How's this?

ADAM   Ahh, the smell of latex. Bastard.

SACHA   How's your mother?

ADAM   My mother? She's fine. She came by last Friday, for her visit. Short and sweet, kind of dull.

SACHA   Oh? *(ironic)* You must be getting along then?

ADAM   Naw, just tuning one another out. I'm not pushing her anymore. She can take her time.

SACHA   That's good.

ADAM   I'll be long gone and in the ground, but she can take her time.

SACHA   *(he stops massaging)* That's a good attitude.

ADAM   You're not the one with the fatal disease.

SACHA   *(up, tearing the glove off his hand)* My life is just as fatal and uncertain as yours, Adam.

ADAM   Oh, don't get academic —

SACHA   The difference is, I'm living my life — what are you doing? Your attitude's driving you down, not the disease.

ADAM   What do you call this? *(as he strikes his own body)* And this? And this?! What do you call the bumps and blisters on my body?! *(throwing off mitts)* What do you call the hairy growths on my tongue, my wasting muscles, my poor, decrepit, aging body?! I watch it every day. I obsess at how it is disintegrating before my eyes. I'm aging a year every week, it feels, and at twenty-eight I'm an old man. I feel death happening, Sacha. I feel it in every pulse of my body, every bend of its creaking knees. *(now striking SACHA)* Every sweat-soaked night. I feel it, and it is terror. You don't. *(grabbing SACHA's neck)* So shut the fuck up.

        SACHA *fights back, pressing* ADAM *to the bed.*

SACHA	Okay, maybe I don't know what it's like. But I live with a constant fear that my brain is going to throw me to the ground for a short, quivering while. Suck out my breath and spit, my eyes blind and wide open, flicking air with my fingers....
	As he says this, SACHA *pantomimes a seizure on the bed.*
ADAM	Stop that. *(SACHA continues)* Stop it, Sacha. Stop it!!
	SACHA *stops. Angry and disturbed,* ADAM *is up from the bed.*
ADAM	Christ!
SACHA	But I get up every day. It's a part of me, I carry it, but it doesn't consume me. Sure, I have epilepsy, but I'm not stuck in bed all day.
ADAM	Good for you, Sacha — just go, this isn't working.
SACHA	Why? I'm not supporting your decline? No, I think it's normal to be afraid and angry, but I'm witnessing you in this, this... willed decline. You don't want to get better, and that's what I can't stand. You have chronic problems associated with HIV-disease. And you spend the whole time in bed wallowing in your sickness. Half your problems are because you don't look after yourself. You're self-fulfilling your destiny —
ADAM	I didn't create this diagnosis.
SACHA	No, but you're not fighting it! Yes, they say HIV leads to death, and you will die. They neglect to say that you might have a dozen years left, probably more. That would put you at forty, Adam. Have you planned for forty? You haven't even planned your next trip to the grocery store!

ADAM Shut up, Sacha.

SACHA I'm serious! Have you thought about *doing* anything? Volunteering? You're on disability now, so why don't you do something with your time?!

ADAM Forget it. Christ, Sash, the worst thing in the world has happened to me. And I can't believe... I don't know how to function with this burden. Every morning as I begin to peel back sleep, this wave of dread and fear hits me like nausea. How can I get out of bed when every morning the knowledge cripples me? This disease has shattered everything I believed about myself. I wanted to show the world what a proud fag could do. And it's as if I got caught and somebody's saying, you fool, what were you thinking? It all seems like shrill hubris now. I come stumbling back home to care facilities and the hypocrisy of family. I don't know why. *(breaking)* She's right, I don't know what I want. AIDS is the worst thing....

SACHA It's not the worst thing in the world, Adam. It's a disease, not a melodrama. Sorry, but it's not the worst. *(pause)* Adam, I....

>*They are close.* SACHA *holds* ADAM's *wrist and looks down.*

ADAM What?

>SACHA *suddenly hugs* ADAM, *who winces in pain, then hugs back, strong.*

SACHA Sorry. Sorry. I'm sorry.

ADAM You're sorry. *(pause)* Your heart's just a-going pitter-pat. What's the message?

SACHA I don't know....

>ADAM *leaves the embrace.*

ADAM	Are you horny?
SACHA	Uh — no.
ADAM	Well, I'm horny.
SACHA	*(unsettled)* Can't help you out on that one.
ADAM	Yes you could. Tina's not around these days, so you might as well get it where you can, while the getting's still relatively good.
SACHA	That's not my... thing.
ADAM	Just as well, you shouldn't touch sixty percent of my body anyway. By the way, I was lying about the blister on my dink — no problem with the mucous membranes. So. It's probably a shitty play. Most theatre here sucks.
SACHA	Oh, does it now. You suddenly an expert?
ADAM	*I've* lived in New York.
SACHA	Oh! Well! You *are* an expert. How can I offer an experience worthy of you?
ADAM	Don't know. But I'd need an aisle seat.
	Sound suggesting airplane. Exit ADAM *and* SACHA. *Enter* MEMORY *and* IRIS. *They sit on the chairs which are now side-by-side, placed by* MEMORY *or perhaps by the men.*

Scene Twelve

                        MEMORY *and* IRIS *are seated.* MEMORY, *right, is asleep. They are on an airplane.* IRIS *looks out the window, left, at the ground below, as if her husband, Cliff, is seated to her left. Confessional.*

IRIS   Clouds came fast, hardly saw the city. *(adjusting the air stream above her)* I better start an exercise programme when I get back from Reno — Cliff says I'm losing *my* shape. And what, I want to know, is "my shape"?

                    Adam's not getting any better here. *(looking out the window)* There. Doesn't want our help, doesn't want my help. But he takes the money easy enough, he does. He is so difficult.

                    A difficult birth, that's what we called it. With his lungs, and born too small. They kept him apart from me so much those first weeks. Because when I held him, he could hardly breathe.

                    Everybody knows. You can tell the way the other women look at me in town, at work. They know my son is gay — but I'm given respect, elbow room. "That woman has come through so much," they say. "She *knows* things we don't." Ha. It's true — I know that Martin and Brenda Fitzpatrick's son, who played rugby and lifts weights, he's just as gay as my son the skinny artist. Just as gay.

At work they'll all be talking about who's getting married and who's having a baby, and I'll come in the room. You can see them cinch up, get careful about what they say all of a sudden. They know. It's just... how do you talk about these things? Walk in and scream "So what?! You get weddings you can invite friends to, you get grandchildren nobody whispers about. Well, your kids are no happier than mine are. Things happen to my kids too, you know. Pretty amazing things that would knock your socks off." But they never ask, no, they never ask. And so I don't say anything. But they know. They remember everything.

Such a small baby, but those first weeks he had such will in him. His face would crease inwards, angry with every breath that shook him. And when I could hold him, it looked like he would burst, hating me almost, for him being here, glaring his dark wet eyes, his fingers' pale wrinkled bone squeezing mine.

He chose to live. That's what the doctors said — he'll choose either way, and there was nothing for me to do but stand on my side of the glass and cry my first tears as a mother. And think, what, my child can *choose* that? Some spark of life in him to say no, not yet. Not yet.

So why now?

> *Suddenly* IRIS *looks up to her right, to an invisible stewardess.*

IRIS Me? Oh, tomato juice. *(to left)* Cliff? What would you like. Beer? *(to stewardess)* Light beer.

> MEMORY *opens her eyes and stretches.*

IRIS Sorry, I hope I didn't wake you.

MEMORY Me? No, I can never sleep.

IRIS *and* MEMORY *continue to sit at the chairs,* MEMORY *slowly dealing cards — fortune teller, card dealer.* IRIS *considers each card.*

SACHA *and* ADAM *appear in different areas, addressing the audience.* MEMORY *and* IRIS *address one another.*

ADAM *(nervous, holding speech notes)* My name is Adam and I'm a volunteer educator. I'm at your school today... to speak. About AIDS. *(to audience)* Who can tell me what AIDS stands for?

SACHA *(at lectern with lecture notes)* Early disease patterns suggest that AIDS advanced in the USA, not Africa. An American disease, made in America.

IRIS Do you play?

SACHA It's a jet-propelled epidemic. But we want to think about diseases happening to others, blame others. Africa. The alien.

MEMORY Black. Jack.

ADAM AIDS is actually a condition. Science thinks it knows the cause — HIV.

MEMORY You plays the game, you takes your chances.

IRIS chuckles.

SACHA In the '70s medical science convinced itself that viral and bacterial infections were a thing of the past.

IRIS I blamed myself.

ADAM This alien parasite invades the body and chooses as its host a specific kind of cell instrumental to the body's immune system.

IRIS	But they said no, there was nothing I could have done.
SACHA	We thought the enemies would be cancer, heart disease, arthritis.
IRIS	He was just born small.
ADAM	And it's damn intelligent.
SACHA	But what happened is, we now have an epidemic that kills through a combination of our most feared and hated diseases — parasites, fungi, blindness, herpes, cancers, dementia, galloping tuberculosis, pneumonia....
IRIS	I blamed myself.
MEMORY	Here's what the cards say.
ADAM	Your colonised body is open to infection, and when you get certain ones, doctors tell you that you have a condition. It is called AIDS.
IRIS	What do they say? He was... different, was gay before he was even born, wasn't he.
SACHA	So. So. History's happening now. It's ours, here. Right in front of you.
MEMORY	It's right in front of you.
SACHA	But we study an epidemic in order to know a society — and looking back, we judge the healthy, not the afflicted.
ADAM	The virus is carried by blood, semen, breast milk and vaginal fluids.
MEMORY	You've carried this with you.
SACHA	And so, ask yourself — what kind of judgment will future societies pass on us?

ADAM   There are three proven ways an adult gets the virus — sharing intravenous needles, unprotected anal intercourse and unprotected vaginal intercourse.

SACHA   Because make no mistake, we will get through this disease. And it will be the healthy, the ones who could do something, who will be judged.

MEMORY   You know what to do.

ADAM   Thankfully, we know how HIV is transmitted.

SACHA   Despite what we know, that the disease mutates faster than any other known virus...

ADAM   Just don't share needles and use condoms, simple.

SACHA   That it is slyly evading a vaccine or cure...

IRIS   Nothing a parent ever could do, right?

SACHA   And that medicine has never stopped or altered the course...

MEMORY   Nothing a parent ever can do.

SACHA   ...of a major epidemic.

MEMORY   *(to* IRIS*)* Ever.

IRIS   *(to* MEMORY*)* Never.

SACHA   Never.

ADAM   No glove, no love. Never.

SACHA   Knowing this, how do we incorporate this contemporary, Western epidemic into our lives?

ADAM   I am a gay man. And yes, I am someone who had unprotected anal intercourse. I have full-blown AIDS. Any questions.... Are there any questions?

Silence while MEMORY *continues to turn cards.*

ADAM   *(as though answering a question)* Yes.

IRIS   Hit me.

SACHA *and* ADAM *throw their papers up into the air. They flutter down across the stage floor.*

All exit, chairs moved off. Lights up low as MEMORY *returns with a large bedspread and places it over the bed, turning to say "Shh!"*

Scene Thirteen

> *While* MEMORY *exits,* ADAM *(as 18) and* SACHA *(as 17) enter* ADAM's *boyhood bedroom.* ADAM *carries a near-empty bottle of red wine. Both carry their shoes. They are drunk, giggly and boisterous.*

ADAM   Shhh! Be quiet!

SACHA   Oh shush yershelf.

ADAM   My parents will hear us upstairs — you wanna wake them up?

SACHA   Yes. Tell them what a bad boy you've been.

ADAM   Shut up — get in here.

SACHA   All right! Jeeze, Adam, lighten up.

ADAM   Sorry. I am. Here, have some more wine.

SACHA   *(drinks wine)* Ooooe, am I drunk. Are you drunk?

ADAM   Yes.

SACHA   Drunk as a skunk. Feels good, doesn't it? My brother says your first time drunk is the best. This is our best, man.

ADAM   Really?

SACHA   Yeah. *(undressing)* Sleeping over here, it's like two years ago, in Grade 10, remember?

ADAM gets into bed, taking off his clothes under the sheets.

ADAM Yeah, sorry there's no extra bed. What do you sleep in?

SACHA I sleep in the nude, man. Don't you?

ADAM Sometimes. Sometimes I... can't.

SACHA How come? Afraid they'll be a fire?

ADAM No.

SACHA So why don't you sleep in the nude?

ADAM I sometimes have trouble. Sleeping. Sometimes it's too hard to fall asleep.

SACHA Ohh, you mean you're too hard, is that it?

ADAM Yeah, that's it.

They both giggle.

SACHA gets into bed.

SACHA Oh, that's a hoot! Man! I usta get that problem too. But ya get used to it. Just put something... COLD on it!

SACHA puts his foot on ADAM's crotch, under the blankets.

ADAM Ooof! Ahh, watch it with the feet!

SACHA Just seeking out the warmest part for my freezing tootsies!

They wrestle. SACHA pulls a muscle in his neck.

SACHA OW!

ADAM	Sorry! Sorry....

Silence, while ADAM *massages* SACHA's *neck and shoulders.*

ADAM	You've got a nice neck. *(pause)* I heard when you're drunk it's harder — I mean, you don't get hard very easily. Do you think so?
SACHA	Hmm. Maybe. I'm kinda hard now though, so I don't know.
ADAM	You are?
SACHA	Yeah. *(pause)* Are you?
ADAM	*(pause)* Yeah.

A long silence broken with giggles and tentative overtures, which build the tension to the point where the only ways forward are either violent or sexual. The silence should suggest the potential for either.

SACHA	I'm drunk, remember.
ADAM	Me too. Are you scared?
SACHA	Nope. We're blood brothers, Adam.

SACHA *kisses* ADAM, *a long kiss.*

ADAM	Wow.

They kiss again. Fade to low light. There is a slow, stylised movement of bodies and blankets as the two of them make love.

After some time, lights come up slow on MEMORY *standing by the lectern. She holds an apple, examining it as she speaks, beginning almost inaudibly.*

> ADAM *and* SACHA *continue their slow movements. She slowly crosses to stand behind the bed by the end of her line.*

MEMORY The substances to which universal precautions apply include blood and other body fluids containing visible blood. The precautions also apply to semen and vaginal secretions. Universal precautions do not apply to feces, nasal secretions, sputum, sweat, saliva, tears, urine and vomitus, unless they contain visible blood. Gloves should be worn for touching... blood and body fluids, mucous membranes, or non-intact skin, for handling items or surfaces soiled... with blood... or body fluids. Gloves should be worn by all persons who are in direct contact with blood, tissue, or body fluids... or particles or surfaces potentially contaminated... by blood... or body fluids. After contact —

> *Lights full up fast on bed.* SACHA *is jolted up, eyes locked open, spit and air exploding through his clenched teeth.* SACHA *is having a grand mal seizure. He quickly falls back to the bed, quivering rigid, his lower arms and hands slightly raised, flicking.*
>
> MEMORY *remains behind the bed. She takes a large bite from the apple.*

ADAM Sacha? Sacha! What are you — ? Oh fuck, Sacha, Sacha! Oh my God, oh my God, oh my God. Mom. *(in panic, he calls)* Mom! Mom! *(beat)* Oh no, no. Sacha, please, please Sacha, stop this. Stop. It's okay. We're gonna get in *trouble*, Sacha. Sacha, what should I do?

> SACHA*'s seizure stops; his arms fall to the bed.*

ADAM There. Sacha, you're okay. Oh, Sacha, I love you.

> IRIS *has entered.* ADAM *turns suddenly to see his mother.*
>
> MEMORY *takes* SACHA *in her arms and carries him offstage.* ADAM, *distraught, wraps the bedspread around him and crosses to the window. Ambulance lights play across him.*
>
> *Lights shift on* ADAM *and* IRIS, *in* ADAM's *bedroom still. Sound of ambulance siren leaving. An accelerated series of events as in one's memories, more about the* truth *of the events than the reality.*

IRIS Christ, Adam.

ADAM You didn't have to call the, the ambulance.

IRIS Nobody takes risks like that. Not in my home. Jesus, what if he died here?

ADAM He wouldn't die.

IRIS So what in Christ's name —

ADAM Nothing. He was *sleeping over.* You said he could. He had a seizure.

IRIS You were both naked.

ADAM We... we'd been drinking.

IRIS You'd been drinking! Doesn't sound like nothing to me, Adam. I can see what's been going on —

ADAM Mom! Sacha's my best friend.

IRIS Adam, shush, I don't want to hear — *(phone rings)* I'll get that. Hold on. *(spoken without miming telephones)* Hello?

> *Lights up on* MEMORY, *at lectern.*

MEMORY	Hello, Mrs. Castorson?
IRIS	Yes.
MEMORY	Is your husband available?
IRIS	No, he's in Ottawa.
MEMORY	Sacha Pollock had a grand mal seizure —
IRIS	Yes, yes, I know this.
MEMORY	As it was his first in nearly two years, and he suffered prolonged disorientation, we ran some tests. We found semen surrounding his rectum. Now there's nothing to worry about with this. About half of all boys have some sex play as children or teenagers.
IRIS	My son is eighteen years old.
MEMORY	Mrs. Castorson —
IRIS	*(panicking)* Now listen to me — I know Sacha, and I know he'd do this, Doctor. He'd lure Adam into something like this. Listen — the reason Sacha was disoriented was he'd been drinking. He was drunk —
MEMORY	Given the evidence, the Pollocks are saying —
IRIS	You should not trust that family. My own son was just saying how he'd been duped by that boy.
MEMORY	Mrs. Castorson, I'm trying to defuse a potentially — and needlessly — explosive situation, and I need your help. Given the evidence, the Pollocks feel, well, it is their opinion that your son... raped their son.
ADAM	Mom?
IRIS	Oh my Lord.

MEMORY	Now we can easily clear things up —
IRIS	Ohh! I will... I will....

> *Lights off* MEMORY. IRIS *turns to stare at* ADAM.

ADAM	What.
IRIS	You. You! *What* are you doing?
ADAM	Mom, what happened? Why did you say that stuff about Sacha?
IRIS	*Did* you?!
ADAM	No, Mom, we didn't do anything wrong!
IRIS	I think I'm going to be sick. Under my roof? In my home. You might as well have killed yourself.
ADAM	Mom, don't say that!
IRIS	Well!
ADAM	I'm sorry — we didn't do anything that bad.... Mom, what's wrong? What did Mrs. Pollock say?
IRIS	That bitch is making terrible, terrible accusations against us. This is going to be ugly.
ADAM	He wouldn't let her do anything bad against me, I know he wouldn't. We're... we're practically brothers, that's all, Mom. I really love him.
IRIS	Shush! That's sick and, and.... And I'll call her in the morning. They'll see this'll hurt them as much as it'll hurt us. I'll fight this, I will.

ADAM   What? Is he — is he *telling* people? Why? It's as much Sacha's fault as mine! He... he started it! Mom, what's going to happen? Are people at school going to know? I can't go back to school if this gets out. I didn't know! I didn't know this was so bad — !

IRIS   You weren't thinking. Sacha put you up to it.

ADAM   What am I going to do?

IRIS   We'll get through. People will forget. There's only two more months of school, Adam. We'll make it. You're okay. Go to bed. They'll forget. People will forget.

>   IRIS *exits.* ADAM *breaks. He looks around himself in despair. Finally, he takes the empty wine bottle in its bag and smashes it. On the bed, utterly distraught, he takes a piece of glass out of the bag, holds it in front of his left wrist, and begins to slice. Blackout.*

               [A secondary although less desirable alternative, if breaking glass is too difficult to arrange, is to have ADAM *use his jackknife, which he finds in his discarded pants pocket.]*

Scene Fourteen

> *Lights up on* MEMORY. *She is tired.*

MEMORY Oh mercy. Bites of an apple, knowledge is.

> *ADAM is in bed, moaning as if in a dream.*

ADAM Sacha... Sacha.

> MEMORY *crosses with bottle and handkerchief to stand behind* ADAM. *She lets fall a small stream of water onto his chest, which jars* ADAM, *as if waking from a nightmare. Lights on the bed shift as they did for* SACHA'S *seizure.*
>
> *Shaken,* ADAM *examines his wrist, tracing a vein in his arm. He grabs the arm as if he has caught something inside.*

ADAM It's inside there. Ticking.

> MEMORY *washes him — chest, face, back — with the handkerchief and water in the glass.* ADAM *does not see or address her.*

MEMORY Your heart.

ADAM A time-bomb pumping fluid that kills me. A stranger.

MEMORY True as the sunset, your blood carries stories.

SACHA *is discovered at the lectern.*

SACHA	The thing is...
ADAM	It's tainted.
MEMORY	It caries your breath.
SACHA	*(moved)* The thing is, in the face of a plague...
ADAM	It's deadly.
MEMORY	It's your life, in daily communion with your body.
SACHA	There's still something ticking....
ADAM	My brother, my own blood, betrayed me.
MEMORY	There was no betrayal.
SACHA	Some reminder of our battered capacities.
ADAM	Why, why was I left like that the first time I loved?
SACHA	But when my theoretical knowledge has never personally been tested...
MEMORY	You took risks of the heart because you couldn't see there were risks.
SACHA	When my memories become a fearsome, mocking hostage...
ADAM	That moment destroyed me.
SACHA	I keep striking bargains with my demons just to keep going on.
MEMORY	The heart won't fail you.

SACHA   There's this... fear in us, pressing up in me. I don't know anymore. There was a cut.

ADAM   *(overlapping* SACHA*)* I have this cut. This cut.... Would you...?

SACHA   And now there's a scar.

MEMORY   What, kiss it better?

Scene Fifteen

        ADAM *in front of a small unfired clay sculpture, wiping his hands with the handkerchief. He has a strong, bright energy.* SACHA *enters.*

SACHA   I brought wine.

ADAM   Two nights in a row? You?

SACHA   Just a glass.

ADAM   Well good. It's a night to celebrate. Where you been?

SACHA   I was working out.

ADAM   *(putting a shirt on)* Working *out*?

SACHA   I started up at the gym again, my end-of-term resolution. I'm getting flabby.

ADAM   I don't think so....

SACHA   Well! It doesn't matter what you think.

ADAM   You looked good last night.

SACHA   When's dinner?

        SACHA *begins cleaning up the room, picking up all papers from the floor, making the bed, replacing the gift blanket on the bed, folding up clothes, and tidying everything.*

ADAM Let's wait and have a glass of wine first. You wanna to go for a walk first? It's so gorgeous out. All these beautiful April bodies budding. Sweaty backs jogging, those tanned calves you can see the veins through. We live in paradise, you know. Hey — we should go camping this summer. Remember we used to go camping when we were kids? Let's do it, okay?

SACHA We need a car.

ADAM Right. Neither of us can drive now. Bummer. Well, we can be innovative. We can camp underneath Lion's Gate Bridge. That's wilderness enough. Honey, we can "camp" down Davie Street. What do you say?

SACHA *(busy cleaning)* Sure.

ADAM See what I've made? I've been playing around mostly, getting the hang of things again. The clay behaves, though, holds to my hands. I close my eyes and I can still do it, I can still make something, blind. Something that stands. I made that with my eyes closed.

SACHA That's swell.

ADAM It's nothing yet, wait till I get going.

He watches SACHA *cleaning up. Tries to reach him.*

ADAM Sash... Sacha....

SACHA I'm hungry, I'm tired and I'm hung over.

ADAM We didn't get much sleep.

SACHA *(turning)* No, we didn't. Listen, Adam, I was drunk last night.

ADAM Yeah, we both were a bit.

SACHA	I know, but... things wouldn't have happened the way they did —
ADAM	If you hadn't been drinking?
SACHA	I don't... I didn't really want to do that. I'm not attracted to you.
ADAM	So, what was last night, then?
SACHA	An indiscretion.
ADAM	*(snapping)* Oh, just like ten years ago. Fine.
SACHA	Adam, I'm not —
ADAM	I know, you're not gay. You keep saying you're not gay — it's your fucking mantra whenever we're together. We slept together one night, can't you just admit it happened? And it was *good*. It doesn't make you any less of a man.
SACHA	I know that.
ADAM	Do you?
SACHA	Look, I know we have a rather... unconventional relationship here. But it's time we set some ground rules.
ADAM	What are you getting at? Rules?! Come on, if you're screwed up from last night, just say it. Let's not worry about what this *means*. It means we are friends and that we care enough about one another to want to express it. Physically. Once. Maybe never again, but what's the point of fencing it off with rules?
SACHA	Because that's the way the world works. I don't want you to deceive yourself into thinking this could be a regular occurrence.
ADAM	Don't flatter yourself, Honey.

SACHA   I'm not, it's just —

ADAM   Look, it was nice getting off. Nice to know I still can. But you know what really mattered? Just giving something to you, Sash. Giving to *anybody* — to give pleasure, create it. It means I'm alive. I'm fine, Sacha.

SACHA   I don't believe you.

ADAM   Well tough shit. You're the one who's messed up, not me.

SACHA   I'm certain about who I am, and *what* I am. I just didn't expect that being your friend meant I'd be forced into being your lover.

ADAM   Oh, did I force you?

SACHA   Not literally, Adam — I mean in the larger picture. You needed that from me.

ADAM   *Don't* you get all pure and righteous. You're suddenly all fucked up just because I'm a man. A minor detail.

SACHA   Look, if you want to know the truth —

           Door knocks. It silences them a beat.
           ADAM *answers it.* IRIS *enters.*

ADAM   Mother? Hello! Ah, gosh, when did you get back from Reno?

IRIS   This morning. Your father —

ADAM   I thought you came back tonight.

IRIS   No, your.... Can I come in? Your father had to pick up some files at the office, so I thought I'd drive him in, and pop by to see you.

           She sees SACHA.

IRIS	Sorry. I should have called first.
ADAM	No, no. No. Um, this is a friend of mine. He's over for dinner tonight. You remember... Sacha Pollock?
SACHA	Hello, Mrs. Castorson.
IRIS	Hel- hello, Sacha. I don't know that I would have recognised you.
SACHA	You're looking swell.
ADAM	How was Reno?
IRIS	Good. Did pretty well at blackjack; came home ahead of the game, actually.
ADAM	Good, good....
SACHA	We were just going to have some wine.
ADAM	Sacha finished his first year's teaching today. We're celebrating.
IRIS	Congratulations.
ADAM	Sacha is forbidden to go onto the campus until September.
SACHA	I have to mark ninety exams.
ADAM	Okay, after you mark the exams, you are forbidden to go to your office. Yes, it's been a very *exciting* day for Sacha, wouldn't you say, Sash?
SACHA	I'll get some wine. I'll be a while.

SACHA exits.

ADAM	Don't pull a muscle.
IRIS	Sorry to drop by like this. I should have called.

ADAM	Yeah.
IRIS	Look, you want me to go?
ADAM	No — I didn't say that.
IRIS	You two have things —
ADAM	Okay, if you want to go, fine, go.
IRIS	You want me to go?
ADAM	No — did I say that? I didn't say that. Stay, have a drink with us. *(beat)* This is bizarre.
IRIS	How are you, son?
ADAM	Can't complain.
IRIS	But do you?
ADAM	Of course. *(they smile)*
IRIS	No pain?
ADAM	Just little things.
IRIS	How are the eyes?
ADAM	*(at sculpture)* Did you win a lot of money?
IRIS	*(pause)* No.
ADAM	Too bad. I was going to ask if you could rent me a studio. You ever come across studio accommodation at the office?
IRIS	Sometimes things come up.
ADAM	Well, let me know. *(pause)* The right one's pretty dim. I let my driver's licence expire. I'm not supposed to watch TV or read very much. You could say I'm rediscovering my sense of touch.

IRIS	What do the doctors —
ADAM	*(of his eyes)* They're going. "Rage, rage against the dying of the light...."
IRIS	My God, Adam, no....

Silence.

ADAM	Come and look at the sun. Mom?

IRIS restrains her emotions, moving beside ADAM at the window.

IRIS	It's sure staying up later and later now. The earth tilting back to the sun again.
ADAM	The fattened calf I slaughtered on the solstice must have helped.
IRIS	*(taken with the joke)* Oh, Adam. *(pause)* You and Sacha...?
ADAM	He's been very kind.
IRIS	Is he... fixed up nice?
ADAM	He's married.
IRIS	Oh!
ADAM	And they're separated. No kids.
IRIS	Oh.
ADAM	He's not seeing anybody. Maybe we should fix him up with Elaine.
IRIS	*(joining in on the joke)* Well, they *did* talk.
ADAM	*(pause)* No.
IRIS	No. *(pause)* It's pretty.

ADAM   I was born at sunset, wasn't I?

IRIS   Yes, I guess around then.

ADAM   Neat. See those clouds? That's what makes a sunset interesting. Without clouds, sunsets would all look like postcards from Hawaii.

IRIS   Not a bad thing.

ADAM   But here, look, the light on them. See the way the light cradles the underside of those clouds? It's... so tender. See? We're getting those rays that shoot out like... like in a bad oil painting, like you could just walk out on a ray to that sun, while it reddens and blushes into the sea. What a collaboration. Do you see?

IRIS   Yes.

ADAM   I missed west-coast sunsets. The sun's more alive here. You appreciate the light more after you've been denied it so long.

IRIS   I think it's the ocean that does it. Did you miss the ocean?

ADAM   Yes. I did.

> SACHA *enters, unnoticed, and stands upstage with wine and glasses.*

IRIS   *(moving away from* ADAM*)* Thought you might. This is a good room, gets good light. Not many have that kind of — *(sees* SACHA*)* Oh! Sacha.

SACHA   Wine?

IRIS   I can't stay long.

SACHA   Tell us about Reno.

IRIS	Well, there's one thing I wanted to tell you about, Adam. Last night? For our final dinner we went out with Ron and Tracy and this other couple. The woman, Mandy was her name, she was such a busybody. This is kind of a silly story, really.
ADAM	No, no. What happened?
IRIS	She started talking about "the nation's" — she's American — "The nation's blood supply" being "at risk." And how we need to protect our blood. How we should — or they should — quarantine AIDS "victims," and how Elizabeth Taylor is just a media-hungry hypocrite who picked the wrong friends in the first place, that's why they're all dying.
ADAM	Well.
IRIS	So — you know what? I told this Mandy that I thought Elizabeth Taylor was the smartest, most generous woman in Hollywood. I told her that only Cuba has quarantine for people with AIDS, and that it's useless anyway. I told her that there's nothing wrong with her nation's fucking blood supply, since they started screening years ago.
SACHA	You're quite knowledgeable.
IRIS	I've been reading. This woman thought you could get it from chip dip — honestly. And Adam, she said people with AIDS deserve to die. I nearly had a heart attack.
ADAM	What did you do.
IRIS	What did I do? I told them. And Ron and Tracy. I told them you had it. That we were your parents, and you had AIDS. You have AIDS.
SACHA	Really.

ADAM	How very brave of you.
IRIS	And Ron and Tracy stuck beside me, they said what a smart, talented boy you are, even though they haven't seen you in ages — which, thank God, they didn't mention. Anyway, it sure shut the Yanks up.
ADAM	What did Dad say?
IRIS	Nothing.
ADAM	Hmm.
IRIS	I bet I impressed him.
SACHA	I bet you did.
ADAM	Cheers. So you've come out.
IRIS	Well, if that's the way you want to put it.
SACHA	Cheers, Mrs. Castorson.
IRIS	Cheers. So, do you live nearby, Sacha?
SACHA	Actually, I'm out by the university.
ADAM	He rooms with me sometimes, stays on the hide-a-bed.
IRIS	Well.... *(feeling friction, finishing her wine)* I hope you have a nice dinner, boys. It certainly has been a long time.
SACHA	Yes, a long time.
IRIS	Time — Oh, I have to go pick up your father. We should have a dinner soon, Adam. Trevor's birthday is coming up. *(to* SACHA*)* Elaine has a son, Trevor. He's turning three. Hard to believe, isn't it? I have to go. *(*ADAM *stands)* Well, we'll be in touch soon.

ADAM	Was there anything...?
IRIS	What.
ADAM	That you came in for?
IRIS	Oh I don't know, to tell you about Reno.
ADAM	Good story.
IRIS	You okay for, uh, money?
ADAM	Sure.
IRIS	Okay. *(they hug awkwardly)* Bye-bye. *(to SACHA)* Nice to see you....

> IRIS *concludes with a silent parting wave, and exits.*

ADAM	My God. Can you believe it? She never asked about my clay work.
SACHA	Christ, Adam, give her a break.
ADAM	What? I just pointed out —
SACHA	She's hardly the witch you made her out to be.
ADAM	I never called her a witch.
SACHA	She's got a lot of guts.
ADAM	Never said she didn't.
SACHA	More guts than you have. I saw her, Adam. She was.... You could have helped her. But you won't budge one inch, will you. *Will* you.
ADAM	I tried. It's hard for me.
SACHA	Yes, of course, it's always hard for you.

ADAM   And you're the paragon of perfectly-integrated self, huh?

SACHA   Me? This has nothing to do —

ADAM   It's too bad *you* couldn't come out.

SACHA   What?

ADAM   Why don't you take a little risk in your life? Risk that you might actually *feel* something for another person.

SACHA   I already took a risk walking through that hospital door and opening your eyes. And that's enough. Now you want me to take on more. Like your mother. She's trying, but you keep changing the rules on her. What risks have you taken, Adam? Life goes on, yours too.

ADAM   Funny how that happens. Ten years ago, I wanted to die, just close my eyes and pour myself into the bed. I wish I could say I've forgotten everything, but I haven't. The memory used to kill me. It's taken HIV in my body and, believe it or not, it's taken you in my life for me to feel life's blood in me again. I'm not well, but I'm not dead. I'm strong. It's the strength of this clay and the huge hunk of turning earth it comes from. But it's also fragile when wrought by another human hand and fired.

SACHA   I'm getting —

ADAM   It's risky handling something like this, Sacha, but not riskier than anything else!

SACHA   I'm getting tested.

ADAM   What? For HIV? Why? *(silence)* From last night?! You're joking. You're the disease professor, you know risk activities as much as I do. We played it safe.

SACHA	You're that sure?
ADAM	You remember, we weren't *that* drunk. We kissed. We touched, held each other. We brought each other off. It was simple, beautiful. No risk activities.
SACHA	You can be so sure?
ADAM	I think I can.

Silence. He is fed up with SACHA*'s trepidation and his own uncertainty.*

ADAM	Fine, go — go get checked.
SACHA	Well, see? You don't know what I should do.
ADAM	What am *I* supposed to do? Stick myself in solitary confinement?
SACHA	No.
ADAM	I wouldn't have done anything that put you at risk, Sacha. Christ, what do you take me for?
SACHA	Something about it. There's something dangerous inside you.
ADAM	You made love with *me*, Sash, not the virus. I am ill, but damn it, I'm alive. Now you want me to act like some chaste corpse?
SACHA	There are things you don't know.
ADAM	Then *tell* me! It's not about what we did, is it? It's about opening yourself up to me. Have you ever had a male friend, a good friend, since me in high school? Have you? You can't be intimate, a friend, with a man, can you? Sacha, come on. You said that you had let the past go, but it's seized onto you these years like a leech sucking blood, and you've got to burn it off.

SACHA   I can't commit —

ADAM   I'm not *asking* for a commitment!

SACHA   Yes, you are, and that's fair. But I can't see my way through this relationship with you, Adam. The risk is that every evening I spend here is one more night I'm not trying to find a *real* life out there — a relationship, career success, a set of friends. I mean, what kind of future can I have with... with another man, when I don't feel... a love for him.

ADAM   Oh Christ.

SACHA   I mean sexually. I don't have a role.

ADAM   Yes you do.

SACHA   Not one I know I can fulfill.

ADAM   It's because I have AIDS.

SACHA   I don't know. I'm afraid that you'll get sick. I'm terrified of that, because I don't know what I'll do. I don't know if I'll be able to stay and care for you. I'm terrified of having to watch you deteriorate. What happens if the pneumonia comes back? I'm more frightened of that than you are. What happens if you can't look after yourself? Or when you go blind? What happens if you wake up in shit and I have to clean you? I can't. I don't think I've got it in me. I've been telling you how much you have to *live*, and look ahead and have joy, but really it's because I'm terrified of that time when you really will get sick again, when you'll need me. I think I'll fail you... again. Christ, what have I gotten myself into?

ADAM   *(sincere)* Who knows?

SACHA   I need to know.

ADAM   Okay. It's simple. If you love me, you'll be there. Hey?

>   SACHA *holds* ADAM *on the edge of the bed. Silence.* SACHA *looks around them.*

SACHA   So little here — just two people, stuck. Together.

ADAM   Together. *(quickly seizes* SACHA*'s arm)* Listen — you want a role? You'd better not falter. I mean this — I need this, Sash. Okay? Okay?!

>   ADAM *looks at* SACHA, *holding his arm tight.*

SACHA   What.

ADAM   I promise... *(taking* SACHA*'s hand, delivered in a tone to encourage* SACHA *to repeat)* I promise...

SACHA   *(flooding)* I promise...

ADAM   To stand by you...

SACHA   To stand by you...

ADAM   Not as a friend...

SACHA   Not as a friend...

>   *Lights slow fade.*

ADAM   Not as a lover...

SACHA   Not as a lover...

ADAM   But as a brother...

SACHA	As a brother...
ADAM	For so long as I may live.
SACHA	For so long... as I may live.
ADAM	There. Will you turn on the light?

Blackout.

The End.